STEPHEN BALLARD
1804–1890

"ONE OF NATURE'S GENTLEMEN"

STEPHEN BALLARD
1804–1890

"ONE OF NATURE'S GENTLEMEN"

An Interpretation by
Pamela Hurle

Stephen Ballard 1804–1890: "One of Nature's Gentlemen"
An Interpretation by Pamela Hurle

Published by Aspect Design 2010
Malvern, Worcestershire, United Kingdom.

Designed and Printed by Aspect Design
89 Newtown Road, Malvern, Worcs. WR14 1PD
United Kingdom
Tel: 01684 561567
E-mail: books@aspect-design.net
Website: www.aspect-design.net

ISBN 978-1-905795-63-5

CONTENTS

ILLUSTRATIONS

INTRODUCTION AND ACKNOWLEDGEMENTS

Ballard is a name very familiar to the people of Colwall, to all interested in the history of the Malvern area and also to railway enthusiasts, engineers and horticulturalists far and wide. Such fame may largely be traced to the life and work of Stephen Ballard who lived from 1804 until 1890 – a long life which spanned unprecedented technological and social change in Britain and throughout the world.

It has long been my aim to write a brief biography of Stephen Ballard. The task was somewhat daunting because I know that such a talented and versatile man still has many admirers in various fields. At last, however, I have decided that I should delay no longer: this is not intended as a definitive biography, but I hope that it will serve as an introduction for readers who know little of Ballard and as a spur for some later author to write at greater length. This is my interpretation of the life and work of a remarkable man.

It could not have been written without access to the diaries and notes of Stephen Ballard, Maria Ballard, Ada Ballard, Fanny Ballard and Fred Ballard. These private papers are the property of the Ballard family, whom I thank for allowing me free use of them. Rosemary Ballard has been particularly enthusiastic about the project, and her late husband Stephen Ballard, grandson of Stephen Ballard the First, spent years in a labour of love collecting the family archive. I also thank Freda Ballard, Marcia Ballard and Lyn Ballard who have generously allowed me to use their family pictures and helped in the reproduction of them.

Unless otherwise acknowledged, quotations are from Stephen Ballard's diaries, originally written in his idiosyncratic shorthand and transcribed by his son, Stephen Ballard the Second.

Above all, I thank my husband for his encouragement and practical help.

Pamela Hurle
August 2010

Stephen Ballard's boyhood home painted by his brother Philip.

I

THE EARLY LIFE
OF STEPHEN BALLARD

In his own words Stephen Ballard *"first appeared in this beautiful world of wonders"* on 5th April 1804 at Ivy House, which still stands at the top of Malvern Link Common. Married in 1795, his parents lived for about 5 years at the picturesque Pickersleigh Court at the junction of Pickersleigh Road and North End Lane before moving up to Ivy House, a small cottage which had been extended.[1] Although the family was middle-class – his father Philip was an attorney – it was not well off. His mother, née Charlotte Baylis, helped to keep the family financially afloat by taking in lodgers, some of whom were very well connected. Young Stephen spent his boyhood wandering through the fields and common land close to his home in an area which had once been part of the great medieval forest usually referred to as Malvern Chase.

---

1.   Hereford Record Office: AW86/3

The Ballard home lay between the extensive properties of two influential families, both of whose empires were centred on Herefordshire estates. The lord of the manor of Leigh was Earl Somers of Eastnor, though at the time of Stephen Ballard's birth the Somers family had not yet built their mock medieval castle. The Foley family of Stoke Edith had bought the manor of Malvern in 1741, and Link Top was part of that manor. It was still undeveloped: what was at first derisively called "Newtown" – shops, churches and neat rows of houses – did not appear there until well into the 19th century.

Back in the 11th century, William the Conqueror had designated land in about 13 parishes to form Malvern Forest, where special laws safeguarded the deer and their environment so that successive kings and their favourites could enjoy exclusive hunting rights. This effectively froze development of the area which was eventually disafforested by Charles I in the 1630s. Much of Malvern Link was in the parish of Leigh which, in 1772, was the first of all the Forest parishes to enclose its wasteland. This took into private ownership land over which generations of local inhabitants had exercised common rights such as the right to graze animals or pick up windfall wood for fuel. Nevertheless, in the early 19th century there were still great tracts of uncultivated land at Malvern Link on which a boy could wander freely and safely. The name "link" – which probably derives from the old English word for gently sloping ground – is ancient and certainly pre-dates coaching times, thus ruling out fanciful suggestions that the name was the result of its being a place where different coach services changed horses and provided a link for passengers to various destinations.

Young Stephen Ballard enjoyed a carefree, open-air life, becoming steeped in the lore and traditions of nature and the countryside. Although he believed passionately in the benefits of such a childhood, he also saw its potential drawbacks, as is shown in his journal:

"lads brought up on common land, free and unrestrained in their rambles, acquire a spirit of independence which, if not corrected and restrained, degenerates into lawlessness."

He could often see both sides of a situation and, looking back in later life, saw clearly both the good and the bad in his father, whose drinking habits caused emotional pain and financial distress to his wife and family of eight children.

"I could relate most distressing scenes that occurred to our household through the poverty which inevitably follows intemperance and want of thrift but these may as well be forgotten."

His grandparents, John and Mary Ballard, seem to have kept the Crown Inn on Belle Vue Terrace in Malvern which may have given his father a taste for alcohol. His father had also lost money in a libel suit. Despite his faults he was perceived by Stephen Ballard as an honourable lawyer:

"an attorney, a profession enabling a man to enrich himself at the expense of others, but this to his credit he never did."

Stephen adored his mother who was

"a good woman most anxious and unremitting in her endeavours to inculcate honest and good principles in her children; she bore up under most depressing circumstances."

To these youthful experiences, perhaps, one may attribute his lifelong desire to foster thrift and temperance in all with whom he dealt.

A romanticised mid-19th century view of Malvern,
showing how little development had so far occurred.

His schooling was far from satisfactory and adds to a large body of evidence that, even when parents paid for it, education in the early 19th century was of very poor standard. Like most people, he was unsure *"when and how he learned his A.B.C."* but believed it must have been at his first school, run by *"an old woman in a cottage below the Cockshot on the Link."* Although its houses are modern, the name of Cockshot Road preserves the tradition of there having been a clearing cut through the forest to facilitate the shooting of game, but it is not clear where exactly the original clearing was made. One hot day, on his way to this school, Stephen Ballard and some other boys took off their clothes and bathed in a nearby pool, refusing to obey the schoolmistress who ordered them to come out. Later on, he briefly attended a school at a shoemaker's at the bottom of the Link. The learning he acquired was not memorable, but a folk remedy for his earache made a lasting impression: the centre of a roasted onion was placed in his painful ear, though its effect is not recorded.

Another school attended by the young Stephen and his elder brother Robert was kept by a man named Lloyd at *"the top of Barnard's Green"*, which probably means the Guarlford Road and was possibly near the ancient elm tree which was a local landmark. Mr Lloyd, who had a wooden leg, did not command the respect of his young pupils. They sat on benches facing him: he was armed with sticks of various lengths with which he hit on the head any boy who appeared to be dozing off or distracting his neighbours. Interminable hours were spent reading and copying from the New Testament or simply sitting quietly doing nothing. It is hardly surprising that, again, very little learning was achieved: the most memorable event was the weekly reciting of, and questions on, the catechism.

Next he was sent further afield to Mr Humphreys' school at Ledbury – *"the best school I ever went to but I was not long there."* Finally he was sent to

> *"the College School, Worcester. All my time there was wasted in endeavouring to learn Latin ... the head master was a clerical gentleman under whom it was my misfortune to be placed. He attended the school about an hour each day, during which time his disagreeable and severe treatment was such as to make him thoroughly hated. At 7 o'clock every morning we boys in our surplices attended prayers in the Cathedral and we generally took our Latin books with us, in order to learn our lessons during the service ... The thought of returning to this school after a long holiday so preyed upon my mind that, on the morning of the day for my return, I stole away from home and secreted myself in the top of a fir tree – then growing in a group at the top of the Link where now is Trinity Church. In this uncomfortable hiding place I remained without food all*

*day. At night I returned home. My parents received me kindly
… I was kindly questioned as to my objection to the school and
related my great dislike of the head master and told of some of
his indecent conduct. I was not asked to go again. Very soon
after, this head master made himself scarce, being accused by
the parent of one of the boys of indecent conduct towards his
son. If all the schools at that time were similar to those that it
was my misfortune to attend, the schools at the present day are
very superior."*

Spending all his time at home, young Stephen was given a flock
of 30 sheep, kept on the Link Common. He tended them carefully
and sold their wool at 2/6d (12½p) a pound. In addition, he
took charge of the family garden and was delighted that his crops
were superior to those of the neighbours. He studied botany and
*"made myself acquainted with all the wild British plants growing
in the neighbourhood."* This enterprising and enthusiastic boy
came to the attention of the Dowager Marchioness of Donegal,
who was one of his mother's lodgers. She secured for him, at the
age of 18, a post at the famous Lea and Kennedy's nurseries in
Hammersmith where, despite his initial reluctance to leave home,
he stayed for over a year, earning 12 shillings (60p) a week.

In the autumn of 1823 he took a position on the Earl of
Plymouth's estate of Hewell Grange, near Bromsgrove. The
pay was less than he had been earning in London, but it was a
good opportunity for him to learn about the management of a
gentleman's estate. It also taught him a lesson he never forgot:

*"I found a difficulty to live and pay my way – and have
often wondered how a man, with wife and family of children
contrived to live on such wages."*

Another reality also had to be faced: he would never have
the capital to set up his own business as a nurseryman, which

was what he yearned for, and he had no wish to be employed in a subservient role by a *"whimsical, tyrannical or otherwise unreasonable employer"*. He decided to turn down the situation obtained for him by the Marchioness of Donegal in the Royal Botanical Gardens at Kew and look for an entirely different career. He had an interest in geometry, a kindly stationer permitting him to pay instalments on a book of Euclid, and he apprenticed himself in 1825 to Henry Lucy, a Cheltenham builder who employed him mainly on carpentry. Before starting work at 6 a.m. he regularly took the opportunity to walk around the town inspecting the carpentry and building being carried out by other workers, becoming almost as passionate about this new career as he had been about botany. In 1827, however, this career also came to a premature end when Lucy could not keep his business going. Ballard's obituary relates *"as an illustration of the vicissitudes of human affairs"* that, long after this, Lucy joined Stephen Ballard's workforce.

After leaving Lucy's employ Ballard was appointed as Clerk to the Hereford and Gloucester Canal Company at a yearly salary of £60 plus rent and travelling expenses. He appears to have owed this appointment to Mr Biddulph, the influential banker who lived at Ledbury Park, the impressive black and white house set in a country estate in the heart of the market town of Ledbury and whose family remained firm friends for the rest of Ballard's life. Mr Maisey, the Canal Company's former clerk, endured a painful death six years later due to cancer under his tongue.

Since the middle of the 18th century canals had become an important means of transport for heavy goods. They were relatively cheap to use as well as being much safer for vulnerable loads such as china, which was often broken when transported by road. Natural rivers had been major trade routes and thoroughfares for centuries; and now the countryside was being criss-crossed by these man-made inland waterways which engineers learned to take through most unpromising terrain. The methods of pioneer canal builders such as Brindley were copied and "navvies", a name abbreviated from "navigators", descended on local communities to dig out the routes planned by engineers who usually had no formal training. Local landowners were happy to make money from the sale of land for canal building, while other investors saw a good return on money which they put into canal companies.

So, in 1827, at the age of 23, Stephen Ballard's life was set upon an entirely new course. With a mind as original and inventive as his, it was to prove a rewarding career, but much hard work, considerable pain and anxiety lay ahead.

II

A NEW CAREER

Although in August 1827 Stephen Ballard came back to the area where he was born, his new career would afford him opportunities for travel at home and, later on, abroad. He had had no formal training as an engineer, but soon became highly regarded for his initiative and enthusiasm, and began to attract the attention of some of the men who were to become famous in the history of transport. This was the period when the drive and talents of one man were enough to see through very ambitious projects. Stephen Ballard was never to receive the acclaim and fame of men like Thomas Telford, Isambard Kingdom Brunel or George and Robert Stephenson, but he certainly became the driving force behind numerous projects, one of which was the completion of a canal from Gloucester to Hereford. It took much of his energy from 1829 to 1845.

Within a year of appointing him as clerk, the Hereford and Gloucester Canal Company rewarded him with a £20 gratuity for *"the zeal and activity with which he executed his office and promoted the benefit of the Company ... and especially for his plan of bringing a supply of water from Canon Frome Mill."*

Although canals provided important transport routes and investment opportunities in the 18th century, in the 19th century serious anxieties beset canal proprietors: railway developers were about to overcome both technical problems and the many prejudices against rail travel. With hindsight it is obvious that railways would soon usurp the position of canals as the most significant and convenient transport for an increasingly industrialised and prosperous nation. The young, enthusiastic and innovative Stephen Ballard had come to the rescue of an already ailing canal company at precisely the moment canals were to be threatened and eventually outmoded. Some of the engineering problems were common to both modes of transport and, indeed, Ballard received a letter from Robert Stephenson in 1828 offering advice on the Canon Frome scheme. He approved of Ballard's plan to bring water to a feeder from Canon Frome but the canal company never carried it out.

The Hereford and Gloucester Company had particular problems, having suffered several setbacks since its creation in the 1790s with the objective of linking the two ancient cathedral cities of Hereford and Gloucester, with a view also to linking Herefordshire to the important port of Bristol. Its first engineer was Josiah Clowes, who died in December 1794. By the turn of the century it had reached Ledbury, from Gloucester, but Clowes' £70,000 estimate for building the whole canal had been insufficient for this work and nothing was yet done to link Ledbury with Hereford. Furthermore, the revenue it yielded was disappointing. In 1829 Ballard was required to report upon the likely advantages and expense of *"taking the canal on to Hereford."* Entrusted with this important task, he had his salary raised to £90 in January 1829. The next 15 years were to see him working long and strenuous days, principally negotiating with landowners and supervising the building of the canal. His original job as clerk evolved into that of engineer and, as his talents became more widely recognised, he acted as consultant engineer on numerous other schemes.

In 1829 the company paid him £25 to go to Liverpool and Manchester *"to see the works carrying on at those places"* – presumably in preparation for the opening of the first passenger railway in 1830. On this excursion Ballard seized every opportunity to find out what other civil engineers were doing. He also seems to have inspected what had been done at Chatmoss by the railway pioneers struggling to carry their line across land so boggy that people could not tread on it. It was a journey full of interest for him, and he did not waste a moment of it:

"I then proceeded along the new road to the slate quarries near Bangor, the whole of which I particularly examined and also the saw mills where the slate is sawn, the machinery for which is very simple and interesting. I next visited that elegant structure, the Menai Bridge; from thence I proceeded over the Conway Suspension Bridge to Chester and examined the new bridge that is now being built over the River Dee. The span is 200 feet which will be the largest arch of stone in the world. The machine for shifting the stone to different parts of the work is very convenient and ingenious. I have made sketches of it and also of other such contrivances as I conceived might ever be useful to me. … I proceeded to Liverpool … walked about ten miles along the L and M and was accompanied by Mr. Stephenson the engineer. … From Liverpool I went to Runcorn to the Duke of Bridgwater's canal and proceeded along the canal 32 miles to Manchester … and particularly examined the Rochdale Canal, the Ashton Canal and the

Bolton Canal and the Mersey and Irwell Navigation. Thence
... towards Worsley Chatmoss ... making altogether about
100 miles of canal that I had passed along. From Liverpool I
returned through Birmingham to Ledbury."

As agreed with the Canal Company, he planned and estimated the cost of extending the canal from Ledbury to Monkhide and thence to Hereford. He reckoned it would cost £53,000, but in the early 1830s, the real extent of the cost in time, energy and money was not clear. The company, however, resolved to apply for an Act of Parliament in order to raise funding, and the work started in 1838–9. Even the negotiations for the purchase of the necessary land were described by Ballard as *"a work of considerable labour – upward of seventy different landowners had to be agreed with."* This is a perennial problem with all forms of transport: both canal and railway builders faced hostility but were spared the national media coverage of controversy experienced by today's motorway builders. Ballard himself was a well respected and conscientious negotiator, and it was as much due to his skills in these areas as to his engineering talents that the plan was eventually realised.

In these early 1830s days of his canal work he still found time for his old passions of horticulture and nature study, and also accepted all kinds of commissions for work. These brought in a steadily increasing income, offered him visits to interesting places and added to his professional experience and expertise. He published a short treatise on tree pruning, strongly advocating that nature knew best and that those growers who pruned their trees were cruelly mutilating them. This treatise was so well received that there was even a suggestion that it might be translated into French. In 1832 he criticised Edward Barrett, father of the poet Elizabeth Barrett Browning. The family lived until that year at Hope End in Wellington Heath, near Ledbury:

"Took a view of Edward Barrett Esq. Pruning in a young plantation at the top of Wellington Heath. The pruned trees were oak that appeared to have been in a most ...luxuriant state. ... The trees would undoubtedly, had they not been pruned, have grown with extraordinary luxuriance."

In 1833 he

"completed a rain gauge made with a glass side to it through which the height of the water may be seen."

He noted hearing the cuckoo on 12th April 1835 and, when surveying in Malvern Wells in 1836, observed some unusual white frogspawn:

"Those little specks that are generally black were of a light straw colour and the jelly part surrounding these specks was very bright and silvery. There was some frogspawn of the common kind in the same water."

Having wide-ranging interests, he sometimes recorded unusual events, such as his attempt to help old Mrs Evans gored by cattle at Powick in September 1836 and given rather short shrift by the landlady of the nearby Lion Inn. Understandably the 1834 discovery by workmen of three skeletons at Dymock fascinated him:

"They lay two feet under the surface of the earth. The first that the workmen came to was broken to pieces before it was observed. The soil was removed from this with more care. They lay nearly at full length with their feet towards the east and their arms folded across their breasts. The skull of one was very carefully removed to see if it had any marks of violence, and it was found that the lower jaw and left cheekbone had both been broken in on one, and on the breast of the other

there was found a piece of iron or steel about six inches long, resembling a chisel more than anything else, much rusted but not all turned to rust. How long the bones had been buried there appear to be no means of ascertaining – some suppose a century or more, others only 30 or 40 years. The back bones were entirely decayed and nearly all the ribs. The bodies were in separate graves all within the distance of 10 or 12 feet. ... On 25th April another skeleton was found, the legs and feet of which were under a hedge at least one hundred years old. ... There is not much doubt but these bodies were buried before this fence was made. ... A piece of iron or steel about 3 inches long resembling the head of an arrow much rusted was found in or near the breast of this skeleton."

In 1834 he attended a course of lectures on Galvanism and Electromagnetism and in London recorded his visit to the National Repository of Arts, where he saw

"Perkins' steam gun discharge a great many bullets in a short time. Saw an electro-magnet that lifted about 150 pounds and electricity obtained from a magnet, the electricity giving a smart shock. Heard an instrument play beautifully – it was worked by a pedal and sounded about 12 trumpets most beautifully."

He also saw the manufacture of chain cables and the use of steam power, noting

"A very simple and efficient contrivance for punching rivet holes through iron plates for the boilers and for cutting with shears the iron. Iron nearly an inch thick could have 17 holes, three-quarter inch diameter, punched through in a minute and was cut with the shears apparently as easy as if it were lead. Saw a boiler for a steam engine being made which when

finished will weigh 27 tons. Saw the works on the railroad from Greenwich to London – this road is on brick arches."

On a later visit to London he recorded riding two and a half miles on this railway in less than 7 minutes for a fare of sixpence. A man of his intelligence must have wondered about the effect that such new techniques would have on transport in general and on the competition with canals in particular. But his enthusiasm for the Ledbury to Hereford canal never seemed to falter.

In April 1836 he spent a few days in Birmingham seeing

"many interesting manufactures: the rivet manufactory, Brass Foundry, the Eagle Foundry, Saw-mills, the Showrooms of Jennings and Betteridge, the Viaduct embankment and excavation on the Birmingham–London Railway. Saw the Town Hall and was at a grand concert held there when I heard Miss Carnforth sing."

Again, the railway was significant and, indeed, he was keen to work on the Bristol–Gloucester railway line. He travelled to London in May 1836 to discuss this with a Mr Walker and his principal surveyor, Mr Courie. Mr Walker's *"time appeared to be very precious"* while Mr Courie was *"a man with very few words and not very polite."* In view of the preoccupations of Walker and Courie, perhaps the most interesting part of his trip to London was seeing in Walker's office a new

"copying press for copying writing, a very excellent and simple machine. … The writing to be copied is laid on a thick piece of paste board then the tissue paper to receive the impression and upon the tissue paper another piece of thick paste board which is oiled and on this a piece of green baize. This altogether is passed through the rollers and back again and the impression is taken."

In July 1836 Ballard returned to the scene of his unhappy schooldays and for a guinea a week *("including the attendance of the servant and cooking")* rented two rooms at 2 College Yard, Worcester. At the town hall he worked on various schemes, apparently drawing up plans for the canal around the Haw Bridge area. On his first Saturday evening in Worcester he walked to Malvern and rode to church at Ledbury on the Sunday. He walked back to Worcester early Monday morning in time for work, but had some fun on Tuesday – two hours at the races and an evening watching fireworks.

In April 1836 he had attended the annual meeting of the Worcester Literary and Scientific Institution, where the mayor of Worcester spoke *"very ably … in favour of the pursuit of science and literature."* Of the many speakers at this annual meeting he picked one as the best orator he had ever heard. Despite those miserable schooldays, Ballard had a most observant and fertile mind, always avid for new knowledge and spilling over with novel ideas.

Weekend visits to Malvern and Ledbury triggered a new idea as he observed a wheat stubble field being ploughed at Wick. He suspected weed seeds were being ploughed into it. In August 1836 he designed a machine to burn the ground: two-wheeled, it would scorch green weeds, burn the stubble and kill off weed seeds, insects and insect eggs. His sketch of the machine is accompanied by the comment *"May be drawn by a stubborn horse and the more stubborn he is the nearer he should be hooked to the fire."* This idea fascinated him but never seemed to be adopted. A more successful invention was his ice-boat, shaped at the front like a pig's nose in order to run water under the ice and break it. This had the potential to solve a major winter problem which regularly caused serious disruption to transport by water, then a key commercial activity.

His scientific and technical interests did not preoccupy his mind so much that he failed to observe the feelings of his fellow men – indeed the skill of careful observation of everything around him was one of his most pronounced characteristics. On meeting an old Scotswoman, he was fascinated by her strong accent and animated manner at meeting old acquaintances. From what he observed he drew the conclusion that *"she is an elderly woman and appears to be disciplining her mind for that change which she seems to be aware must take place before long."* But this was the musing of a young man – he himself remained active right to the end of a long life (86 years) and might have put a different interpretation on the Scotswoman's attitude to death when he became older.

Little may be deduced of his social life from his diaries, though occasional comments suggest the usual interests of young men. When working near Gloucester one Sunday evening he

> *"went to Mr Murrells where I stopped till after ten o'clock. Took supper there and spent a very pleasant evening. The two Miss Murrells very lively, good humoured, tolerably good looking girls – was much pleased with their company. Returned to the Dog Inn where I slept and on Monday 29th August 1836 worked on the plan of Overbury."*

The next Sunday was spent in much the same way, and he even *"lent Miss C. Murrell the first volume of 'Pursuit of Knowledge'."* The following weekend he went to see Mr Biddulph, his old banker friend in Ledbury. They discussed a proposed railway to Hereford, and Mr Biddulph, who had supported him from the time of his appointment to the Hereford–Gloucester Canal Company, remained convinced that a canal between Hereford and Gloucester would be more practicable. The proposed engineer of the Gloucester–Hereford railway was Mr Price, and Ballard discussed with him at The Feathers in Ledbury the best route for the railway to take. *"On this day I was particularly well, had a good flow of spirits and felt quite different to what I generally do."* This is a clear indication that Ballard was not a very happy young man. He was sometimes troubled by toothache and possibly suffered physical discomfort from some other non-specified illness – one possibility is chronic sinusitis, though low blood pressure has also been suggested as the culprit. Despite his good spirits in Ledbury, he seemed to have upset his sister-in-law by his failure to acknowledge that her newborn son was *very pretty ... she was almost angry for ... not seeing or saying I saw his beauty."*

At the beginning of October 1836 he had an accident on the way back from Hereford, when the back wheels of his chaise came off after a collision with a wagon carrying stone. *"We tied the wheels under the chaise and rode safely to Ledbury, taking tea at The Foley Arms Inn, Tarrington."* Accident and remedy were both rather different from mishaps on today's roads.

In October 1836 he started work, going on till late at night, in a *"comfortable room prepared for my use"* in offices in Foregate Street, Worcester, continuing to produce various cross-sections for use at Kempsey Bay on the Worcester canal. On 20th October he attended at Worcester Museum a lecture which confirmed his distrust of formal education. An advocate, Mr J. Simpson,

> *"spoke very decidedly against the education that is afforded at schools and colleges – and of the usefulness of the Classics, as they are called. Against these dead languages, Greek and Latin, as they're taught – both languages of barbarous nations. Both the Greeks and Romans were barbarous as compared with the standard of civilisation which he should explain and describe – and their works not calculated to afford that instruction that a rightly educated person ought to have."*

The lectures by Mr Simpson continued over several evenings and caused Ballard to confide to his own journal views which have a surprisingly modern ring. They should be read in knowledge of the fact that the Victorians did not give up the spectacle of public executions until the 1860s. Until that time it was considered suitable for the public – including children – to witness these terrible events. George Turberville, a Worcestershire chronicler, graphically described several executions in the early 19th century at Worcester's new prison, built in the style of a castellated building. Incidentally this caused the fanciful name of Castle Street to be given to the road formerly known more authentically as Salt Lane, it being the route taken by salt traders from Droitwich. After listening to Mr Simpson speaking not only on education but also on capital punishment Ballard wrote:

> *"He in the most able manner advocated the utility of infants schools. … His principles of education actually coincided with those I have for some time had. But I was most of all pleased at finding him opposed to our treatment of criminals and that he is decidedly against destroying human life for any criminal not even for murder. These human notions set forth by so able an advocate as he is cannot fail to extend and become much more generally adopted than at present. I have long ago been decidedly against the horrid, cruel and inhuman practice of taking away the life of a fellow creature for any crime, but can find very few that agree with me. Most stick out that it is right to hang for murder."*

Worcester may have been only a provincial town, but political feelings ran high in it. The week of Mr Simpson's lectures also saw more than 1400 tickets sold for the great reform dinner on 24th October, and a great procession went up and down Foregate Street. The 1830s were the period when the new

Whig government, elected in 1832, launched a comprehensive programme of change and reform in poor law administration and in central and local government. It also saw the beginnings of government intervention in many fields hitherto regarded as matters in which private rights took precedence over all other considerations – education, factory conditions, postal services and the compulsory registration of births, marriages and deaths. The registration of these key life events was the only means of giving teeth to some of the other reforming legislation. Ballard passed no opinion on these matters, but chose to record rather more mundane affairs such as a visit by his cousin,

> *"P. Baylis called at my lodgings. … I did not see him and he left neither note nor message which I think rather strange, but I heard he came by coach with a young lady and she most likely took up most of his time and attention."*

Although unwell on 23rd October Ballard was pleased to meet Sir Thomas Warmington, *"a plain straightforward man, not at all like the generality of gentlemen."* His son was also present and Ballard thought him

> *"a very superior young man … just returned from the continent. He spoke of the buildings abroad and seemed to be fond of architecture and from the remarks he made I should think he has good taste. I felt unwell this day and was angry with myself for being so stupid."*

Ballard nearly died on 5th November 1836, when a sudden gust of wind overturned the boat from which he was taking soundings in the river, probably near Ashleworth. He tried to swim for the bank but got caught up in the boat's landing line:

"I put my hat with the brim down in the water before me thinking to help to keep myself up – but this was of no use to me. ... I went under water, was put out of breath but shortly recovered and swam regularly but here again the ropes interfered. I could not swim to the boat; I caught a foot board or structure that was floating and put it under my breast in hopes it would help to keep me up. ... At last J. Price held out a sounding rod which I caught hold of ... till a small boat could be brought up from Ashleworth. I had on a great coat and had certainly a very narrow escape of my life.

Ballard was in demand for work in places such as Dudley, Stourport, Wolverhampton and Stafford. So long as such commissions did not interfere with his duties for the Hereford–Gloucester canal company, it was happy for him to undertake them. On one of his many journeys he was intrigued to see

"Churches steam coach on common road in Birmingham. It is a very large carriage and was travelling at not less than 9 miles an hour. ... A number of persons were on it."

By now he was becoming quite keen to get himself known. Mr Biddulph of Ledbury urged him to visit his son in Wales *"not that I should be paid for more than my expences of the journey but he thought it would introduce me and make me known."* He also noted that the Institution of Civil Engineers had published in its report a letter he had written on the subject of lock gates without ironwork. This, together with his work on the ice-breaking boat, led to his being elected an Associate of the Institution of Civil Engineers in 1837 – the year of Queen Victoria's accession. By now he was able to command the not insignificant fee of one and a half guineas (£1·57½p) a day for consultancy work. He sent his mother £20 in January 1837, though such a very generous gift did leave him rather pressed for money for a while.

He became particularly involved in 1836–7 with work for the Severn Navigation Company. The supervising engineer was Thomas Rhodes, from whom Ballard took instructions on various surveys of the riverside land and the flow of the river. In December 1836, in order to inspect the effects of flooding, he walked from Gloucester to Upton. The main aim of the Company, however, seems to have been to get a bill through parliament that would enable it to improve the navigability of the River Severn so that ships, rather than small boats and barges, could use it.

Very often his technical reports are enlivened by the continuing observant comment of the countryman. In February 1837 he went to Frampton-on-Severn and

> *"saw the tide come up. A very grand sight, the water ran in all directions at the same time with great force. The banks below the pool are wearing away very fast. The land belongs to Lord Seagrave. He is putting a great coating of stone to protect the banks. Saw thousands of wild geese which are preserved by Lord S."*

A little later,

> *"Saw several barberry bushes growing on the hedge near Whitminster, apparently wild. Thrushes singing beautifully at Frampton."*

On another occasion, at Mr Biddulph's home he met a man who said

> *"print kept better in the dark than in the light and he had heard that if a tadpole were kept in the dark it would grow to an enormous size without turning to a frog."*

In March 1837 he was offered a six month contract by Mr. Biddulph's son who was building a railway in Wales and had already received plans for bridges designed by Stephen Ballard. Mr. Rhodes at the Severn Navigation Company was reluctant to let him go, but Ballard was already somewhat disenchanted with Rhodes, who had been tardy in recommending him for associate membership of the Institution of Civil Engineers. Other offers also came his way, bringing him to the attention of several of the local gentry. Mr Dowdeswell, of Pull Court near Tewkesbury, was installing a reservoir and pipes to provide a water supply at his home and, after Ballard spent several days advising on the best method to do this, went on to discuss with him the long-standing issue of the drainage of Longdon Marsh. He also asked Ballard to design a new carriage road to Pull Court, a project supervised by Ballard in the ensuing months. Mr Watson, land steward for Earl Somers at Eastnor Castle, which had been built in 1812, invited him to go and see the saw-mill at Bronsil, on the Eastnor estate. Mr Biddulph continued to urge Ballard to work on his son's railway undertaking in Wales, though cooled a little after Ballard asked for £9.9.0 a week, with £2 a week extra for his brother Philip.

Eventually they arrived in Wales and took a cottage *("very dirty and scarcely any furniture")*. Ballard was quite unequivocal in his views of Wales:

> *"The cottage where Philip and I are to work and live is so very dirty it is miserable to be in it and the Welsh folks are generally very dirty. They charge most extravagantly for what they do, are filthily dressed, lazy and poor."*

A nearby village he dismissed as *"a filthy place filled with drunken men and women."* It was perhaps as well that his contract was on a very temporary basis: he dined with Mr Biddulph, Junior, and *"told him I wished to leave the country as soon as possible."* He was back in Herefordshire within the month and decided that the letter he received a fortnight later from Mr Biddulph, Junior, had been *"written when he was in a bad humour"*. He refused an offer made a little later to go back to Wales and had great difficulty in getting proper payment for his work for the Welsh railway company. Eventually, in May 1838, he reluctantly accepted £50 instead of the £79 to which he believed himself entitled. On accepting the £50 he wrote of the Llanelly Railway Committee,

> *"I hope the lesson I have had from the rascals comprising this Committee will be of service to me in making my agreement with any other committee or company, for I have been used by them in a most shameful manner."*

For many days after his return from Wales he worked hard at the Pull Court water supply scheme, resulting in his suffering more of the head-aches of which he often complained. But at last *"the water was turned into the pipes yesterday and reached the reservoir at the top of the house in one minute."* Even in the thick of all his plans, his countryman's interests helped to put things into perspective and gave him some light relief: he found the grasshoppers on the Herefordshire Beacon were *"of an endless variety of colour, some of them very beautiful."*

In August 1837 he went off with two others on a railway journey to Liverpool. They *"took seats on the outside of the carriages and was much annoyed by the dust from the engine; it got in our eyes."* One of the many widespread objections to railways was the fear that the noise and speed of trains would cause cattle to abort. When Ballard made this memorable train journey he made the point that *"the cattle in the fields near the railroad took no notice of the carriages, not even when they were quite near to the road. About 200 passengers were on the train."* He was, however, quite ill for a week after this adventure and was obliged to turn down an offer to go to Ireland on business. Having insufficient work to do made him particularly depressed, and for several weeks his diary is peppered with the word *"head-ache"*, though there is still no clearly defined cause of the problem. His social life seemed to be improving, as he took up quadrille dancing in the autumn and *"spent many very pleasant evenings at it."* He was also satisfied that his "scorcher" and ice-boat had proved successful. Indeed, on 11th January 1838 he took the latter to *"liberate 4 boats"* which had become trapped in ice. That year started with very cold weather and he made frequent reference to using his ice-boat. On 13th January at Dymock the ice-boat *"drawn only by two weak horses"* broke up ice that was four inches thick.

> *"A great many persons came to see her and expressed themselves as much pleased and surprised at the easy way she broke up the ice. After having performed a journey of 32 miles (from Ledbury to Gloucester and back) she was examined and found to be quite uninjured."*

Stephen Ballard's ice-breaking boat.

The basic boat may be used for several purposes but when used as an ice-breaker the ice-breaking frame [A] is attached to the front of it. The wooden boat is cased in iron and the whole contraption is quite large. Of the three projecting poles the central one is 31 feet long and the two outside ones are 27½ feet long. A heavy timber [C] weighing about one ton is attached by a chain to the spar B, its weight preventing the back of the boat rising when the front of the boat pushes against ice. The thin shaft [h] enables the boat to be steered by a man walking on the tow-path. Men may also stand on the rear part of the platform between the two cross-pieces [e and c].

Ice of 6 inch thickness also presented no problem but on January 17th seven inch ice defeated the ice-boat. However, use of 3 or 4 horses subsequently enabled the boat to break up ice of thickness up to 18 inches and was clearly a great success, reported in local newspapers. By contrast, another team in Worcester had tried, without this invention, to break up ice and *"it was said that it cost them £40. They kept on till they tore 3 boats to pieces."* On 25th January 1838 he wrote that he *"went to the Institution of Engineers and received the Telford Medal for my boat."* The coveted Telford Medal was awarded in memory of the eminent engineer Thomas Telford, first President of the Institution from 1820 until his death in 1834.

As was his custom, Ballard walked long distances, apparently thinking nothing of walking, for example, from Leominster to Ledbury, a journey which left him *"not much tired"* in April 1838. The next month he walked to Ledbury from Hereford and admitted to being very tired, though this may well have been due to several consecutive days working at *"levelling the Gloucester to Hereford Canal."* In fact, his health was often poor and he complained of a very sore throat. A touching reference to his mother suggests that he was probably also extremely lonely:

> *"Mother spent much time with me, and showed that affection which I never experience from anyone else."*

His social life was circumscribed by his strong moral beliefs. In August 1838 he mentioned the races at Ledbury:

> *"did not go near them as I considered that they ought not to be supported on account of the fighting and drunkenness which is encouraged there."*

He endured poor health for much of 1838. He was *"vaccinated in both my arms"* in July and a fortnight later *"was far from happy in my mind"* as a result of having *"idled my time away"* on a visit to his Uncle Philip. He clearly felt a passionate need to keep busy and by November was in a deep depression:

"This serious illness will, I hope, if ever I recover from it, make me … careful to preserve the blessings of health if I should again have them."

His loneliness was reinforced in February 1839 when his brother Robert left the home they shared in Ledbury to marry and live in the Southend, a short walk away. *"I am now living by myself."* But he saw plenty of people when in March he supported one of Victorian Britain's most lasting reforms:

"took a petition round the town for signatories in favour of the uniform Penny Post."

In the same month, in London, he saw the neo-gothic buildings so familiar to us today which replaced those destroyed by fire in the 1830s:

"viewed the New Houses of Parliament which are being built."

In August 1839 he moved to another house in Ledbury's South Parade. A libel action taken against his father by Mr Archer of Malvern further distressed him, and his lawyer sent in a bill which Ballard thought excessive.

"He would only take off £4, said he charged as low as he possibly could, which I did not believe. He is like other lawyers, will say and do anything for money."

By 1839 he had worked for the Canal Company for 12 years – much longer than had originally been envisaged. He felt himself entitled to a salary increase, and in October was offered the high figure of £400 a year, including house rent and travelling expenses. The first person to be told this good news was his mother, who still faced family problems with the seriously declining health of her husband. Stephen Ballard was to find that the money would be hard earned – and there would certainly be no immediate cause for him to feel guilty or depressed that his time might be *"idled away."*

III

FINISHING THE CANAL

Today we hear frequent complaint at how computers and emails increase stress levels; similarly Stephen Ballard found the advent of the penny post in 1840 increased his work load enormously. But it is even more significant that work on the Hereford–Gloucester canal intensified from the spring of 1840. The hard labour was very occasionally enlivened by some unusual event, such as the discovery in April of *"a great many human skeletons while sinking for gravel in hilly ground near Prior's Court."* In April he paid out £380 in wages to 500 men. In May it was common for digging to start at 4 o'clock in the morning and go on well into the evening. On 1st May Ballard got back to Ledbury at 9.30 p.m. and fell asleep over his meal. The wages bill continued to rise and by July he found himself *"too much occupied to write diary, all time and thoughts are engaged in Canal business."*

He did, however, attend meetings of the local turnpike trust on 26th June and also in November. Clearly he took an interest in all forms of engineering and in the fortunes of those engaged in building and maintaining the best roads to be found in Britain since Roman times. Presumably he could also see the threat to canal investors, already beset by rival railway companies, of competition from yet another mode of transport which had been transformed by the development of new techniques.

Even the long summer days were insufficient for Ballard, who wrote on 23rd September:

> "*If I had ten times as much time I could spend it all on the works which I take pleasure in.*"

His parents remained very important to him and he was pleased to be able to persuade them to come on 18th November for the winter, even though he had "*a brisk argument about religion with them*" within the week. He held firm opinions, too, on drink, recording a "*strong argument with Mr White on the use of alcohol*" a few months later. In December he heard a rumour that he was "*playing into the hands of my brother in allowing him to supply the bricks*" but the matter seemed to blow over. He was concerned to find when doing his personal accounts in January 1841 that he had spent £410 in the previous year and resolved that he "*must be more economical this year.*"

By now he had invented several machines – the scorcher, a screw paddle and boats propelled by air forced against the water – only to see other men take out patents for similar devices. His friend and patron, Mr Biddulph of Ledbury Park, was still keen "*to do something for me, in bringing me forward.*" But he really seemed unable to fit all his activities into his busy life. The purchase of land for cutting and laying later stretches of the canal needed his attention, with 54 landowners being involved in the stretch between Canon Frome and Hereford. The actual canal works, which he preferred, also demanded his attention. He became so desperately short of time that he decided not to waste it by going home at night, and set about building at the Ashperton tunnel a temporary house to which he removed some of his furniture. In the middle of all this, Mr Dowdeswell asked him to examine the water supply at Pull Court, though this seems to have been a welcome respite from the canal business. It hardly seems surprising that by August he spent a week with violent headaches and toothache. Resentment also set in *"Much overdone with work. I think it curious that out of all my numerous relations not one should come and help me move and arrange my things."*

He was also irritated by the *"stupidity"* of his relative Baylis, who seems to have been a foreman: *"a large stream of water was running down the slopes of the cutting into the Canal tunnel."* The mishap required 5 men and 5 horses to pump it out continuously and kept Ballard from his bed for a whole night. On 14th October another accident occurred and he did not get to bed until 1 a.m. as he had to stay with a boy who fell 60 feet down a shaft. In November he had to go to Over, near Gloucester, because a lock gate was broken and lost in the River Severn. He spent what was left of the night in The Dog Inn:

"From Ashperton walked into Ledbury, took a carriage and drove to the Dog Inn where I arrived at 2 a.m. At 6 a.m. went and examined the lock … returned to Ashperton to attend the canal meeting and went back to Ledbury at night."

Nor did the weather help. By the end of November,

"The exceedingly heavy rains are doing us considerable damage, hindering the work and causing serious slips."

In his 1841 end of the year survey, having lived for months at his house in Ledbury's South Parade and in the temporary house at Ashperton, he wrote,

"This year I have been very much engaged. Not a single day, not even Sundays, have I been disengaged from the work of the Canal. To look back to this time last year, it appears an immense long time."

It went on and on. By March 1842 pay day was *"the highest we ever had. £650."* In April he wrote *"Since this job has been on I have made 16 hours a day and feel tired when I get home at night."* His employers seem to have valued him, praising his industry in promoting the interests of the Company, though in the mid 1840s he became disenchanted with it and was also deeply disappointed not to have been made county surveyor when the position fell vacant in the summer of 1842. He did not, however, object to long hours of work, nor even to repeated crises when slips of land threatened canal work that had been done. Indeed, he scorned those who did not work hard, being moved to comment after his brother Philip took his wife

"to Ledbury to see the American Riders perform. I do think that the principal object of a woman's life is pleasure, they are always seeking it and most of them think of nothing else."

All his life he enjoyed work and thought it a vital part of happiness, but in the 1840s he seems to have become obsessive about it. In September 1842 the Canal Company held a meeting, after which,

"Mr Biddulph came and very kindly recommended that I should have a good long holiday, my health required it and I deserved it. I thanked them but rather declined on account of the fear of the company's interest suffering by my absence."

As the canal progressed he gave up his temporary shelter at Ashperton and divided his time between his Ledbury house and what he called "the Nutshell" at Canon Frome. But things were not going well, and 70 men had to be laid off in November 1842. Heavy rain caused land slips and he slept all of one night by the fire in a chair, fearful of what damage might be done. Money was running out, too, so the next day he had to go to Birmingham to try – in vain – to borrow £13000, without which the canal could not be taken beyond Canon Frome. After this he went by rail to Tewkesbury *and was much pleased with the regularity and comfort of railway travelling.* It is impossible to believe that such an intelligent man did not entertain very serious doubts about the future of the canal system into which he had poured so much of his energy and talent. Further bad news was the death of his father at the end of November: the old man was buried near the south door in Ledbury Church.

By the spring of 1843 Ballard's health was clearly poor. In April he had

> *"very violent inflammation in my eyes, bad headache and very ill … Dr. Cooke came and put on 11 leeches which gave great relief."*

By May he was asked to give evidence at the House of Commons concerning the traffic in coal. His circuitous route involved a market boat to Ledbury, a carriage to Worcester, a train to Birmingham and then another to London, where he arrived at 5 a.m. He spent two days at the House of Commons but his evidence was not taken. Instead, he *"had likeness taken"* – an early photograph – and then returned to Malvern before going over to Canon Frome for more canal work. Two gold rings and an old coin had been found and Ballard gave them to the bishop when he saw him in Hereford. He also heard the famous speaker Cobden speak in Hereford on the subject of the Corn Laws – *"his arguments seemed unanswerable."*

The Skew Bridge at Monkhide
(photograph by Bob Embleton © and reproduced with his permission).

About this time, too, new investments in the Company enabled work to continue. At Monkhide Ballard designed an extraordinary "skew bridge", built in 1843 at an angle of more than 60 degrees in order to cope with existing roads.[1] Bick suggested that such a construction was due to *"Ballard indulging in a display of technical virtuosity."*

In October he went to Liverpool to attend a sale of cranes and also tried to buy one in Birmingham, managing to do so at the end of the month. The whole of the year was punctuated with bouts of ill-health, usually referred to as *"headache"* – he must have been very unhappy but, verging on 40, still considered himself a young man. On Christmas Eve he went to Birmingham and the next day, there being no coach, he *"took a fly to Malvern with two other young fellows, and walked on to Ledbury."* By

1. David E. Bick, *The Hereford and Gloucester Canal and the Gloucester–Ledbury Railway,* p.26–8, The Pound House, 1979.

the end of the year he was looking forward to a dance on 2nd January 1844. In February some recognition of his achievement was at last forthcoming. Although the canal had so far been completed only as far as Withington, the canal company wanted to pay tribute to his endeavours of the last few years, which had increased traffic on the canal, and thus added to the receipts of the company. He was to be guest of honour at a dinner at the City Arms Hotel in Hereford. The jollifications started in Ledbury when two packet boats with over 70 passengers went by canal to Canon Frome Wharf, where they were joined by another 27 boats with a further 130 passengers, including a band, and various merchandise, including coal, timber and salt. The whole party went to Withington where the church bells

> *"sent forth their merry peals, which accompanied by the discharges of artillery and the spirit-stirring naval air 'Rule Britannia' by the band had a very pleasing effect."*

Five hours after the 9 a.m. departure from Ledbury there were about 3000 people who had joined in the celebrations, many arriving at Withington on foot and in carts. The leading participants, including Stephen Ballard, went in stage coaches to Hereford, where the bells of All Saints' Church pealed out to welcome them. Two hundred sat down to a dinner which started at 5 p.m. and ended at 10 p.m. They heard many speeches in praise of canals in general and Mr Ballard's in particular. All were full of praise for his skill, industry and integrity. The chairman, F. H. Thomas summed it up:

> *"I need not enlarge on the advantages of a ready and cheap communication by water. It carries to the best market, at the least expense, the corn and cider of the tenant, and the bark and timber of the landlord. It brings to all that necessary of life, in this climate, coal of a superior quality to that with*

which we were heretofore supplied. ...Though at present some complaint might be made of the state of our roads, they must be eventually benefited by the transfer of all heavy carriage to the Canal. For all these benefits we are mainly indebted to an individual, to pay respect to whom we are this day assembled, who has planned and executed the line of the Canal with great professional skill, and whose zeal, upheld by exemplary patience, and aided by kindness of manner and the well-earned reputation of strict integrity, has conciliated the many conflicting interests in the course of the canal, and, triumphing over every obstacle, has reached its present temporary limit. I have the honour of proposing the health of our respected guest, Mr. Ballard.

The *"temporary limit"* was only too painfully obvious: the Gloucester–Hereford canal did not go as far as Hereford, whose mayor was honest enough to admit at the dinner that *"the Council and Citizens have not, I regret to say, aided and assisted much in bringing the canal to Hereford."* Others also criticised the inhabitants of Hereford who had *"shown such apathy"* whilst *"their neighbours in the smaller town of Ledbury had ... originated the canal, and by the support they had given to it, had been a principal means of conducting it to its present terminus. ... the citizens of Hereford owed a large debt of gratitude to the inhabitants of Ledbury."*

Stephen Ballard, in replying to the toast to himself, pointed out that he was about to take up residence at Withington, in preparation for the work on the final four mile stretch to Hereford. Possibly stung by criticism made about the citizens of Hereford at the dinner, investors came forward, as Ballard recorded in his diary for 15th April. But he was personally depressed by the ill health of his brother Thomas and also because trade on the canal was not up to his expectations. Uncertain what he would do when at last the project was completed, he was now well aware of the threat of the burgeoning railway network.

> *"In extremely low spirits, vexed at the affairs of the Canal. The trade does not go well, we have very little work to do to complete and the Railways are coming in on the north and south.*
>
> *In very low spirits about the bad prospects that surround our canal. Railways everywhere and no funds to complete our little work."*

He had been connected with the canal company for 17 years and eventually decided that he wanted to give up his work for it. But it was reluctant to let him go

> *"in the present unfinished state of the canal ... unless a sufficient portion of [his] time could still be occasionally guaranteed for the general superintendence of the Canal for such is the opinion of the Committee as to Mr Ballard's integrity of purpose on all occasions that they readily leave to himself the determination of this question."*

Ballard announced that the canal would be opened in May 1845 – and it was. He and his Uncle Philip let the water into it *"witnessed by not one single person out of Hereford."* Having seen *"the lifting of the planks"* he *"then rode off home."* On 22nd May he

> *"had the satisfaction of seeing the water turned into the basin at Hereford. ... it was contrived that I should see it before I started for London. I was greatly affected at leaving Withington. It was a fine morning and the country looked beautiful. I could not refrain from shedding a tear, near 18 years I have been employed on the Canal and my spirits dropped when the hour arrived for my leaving it."*

The next day Stephen Ballard started on a new project. It was the other side of the country at King's Lynn, where he was to become resident engineer of the Middle Level Drain in the Fens – a task which justified his promotion to full membership of the Institution of Civil Engineers in 1846. His comment on 14th March 1846 proves his realism in entering new employment in the fen district:

> *I continue to have very poor accounts of the Canal. The receipts are not enough to pay even the interest of the borrowed money. This is a most unfortunate affair and the low income may be attributed principally to the projected railways preventing anyone from embarking in the trade of the Canal. Everything seems to tend to wean me from Herefordshire."*

IV

THE MIDDLE YEARS

Whilst Stephen Ballard suffered some of his most unhappy years during the 1840s, those years also saw some of his most rewarding moments. The Canal had cost him much in terms of work, frustration and health but he was justifiably satisfied by its completion. Similarly, his years on the other side of the country would bring him considerable pain and some long-term rewards. From his arrival in the middle of 1845 he felt great loneliness, exacerbated by news of the death on 14th February 1846 of his beloved mother, Charlotte, whom he had always considered his greatest support and friend. His social life in the Fens seems to have rather stilted and left much to be desired. On 1st August 1847

"The Rev. Mr Birch sent me a present of a hymn book and a cucumber which I considered a very polite attention"

and the next day,

"I feel rather in want of company especially as our work is not going as fast as I wish."

By Sunday 14th November 1847 he was clearly feeling very sorry for himself:

"Spent rather a dull day, not a person to speak to and I form but a poor opinion of the people of this neighbourhood. They seem to have no kind feeling."

He toyed, as he had done before, with the idea of marriage and eventually met the woman who would become his supportive and devoted wife for the final 36 years of his long life. Work in the Fens on the Middle Level Drain brought him into disagreement with both the contractors, who were uncooperative, and the workforce, who were not always reliable. He felt himself to be underpaid, and started to consider seeking work with a famous engineer such as Brunel or Stephenson. In 1847 he began an association which would ensure his financial security.

Some interesting encounters must have taken place at the railway station serving the ancient university town of Cambridge. It is claimed [1] that one of them was the meeting between Stephen Ballard and Thomas Brassey, one year younger than Ballard and already famous as the contractor for numerous railway lines, such as the London–Southampton and Paris–Rouen lines. His work covered many countries on continental Europe and by the time of his death in 1870 he had achieved fame throughout the world, having worked in Canada, South America, India and Australia. In the late 1840s Brassey was contracted to make the section between Biggleswade and Peterborough of the Great Northern line from London to the north. He faced an apparently insoluble problem on the route – a *"quaking bog"*, 3½ miles wide and

---

1. *Malvern Advertiser,* 22nd November 1890, Obituary of Stephen Ballard.

nearly ten miles long at Whittlesea Mere. Seeking a solution, he was advised to make contact with Ballard because of the latter's experience in the Fens.

Ballard's journal records numerous meetings with Brassey, the first in March 1847 when he *"had a great deal of talk with the great engineer."* Six weeks later Brassey was prepared to *"talk with me about an agreement to superintend the work, he behaved very politely and agreeably."* On 10th June Ballard

> *"Went with Mr Brassey to London and as we went in a railway carriage by ourselves we had a good opportunity of talking over the subject of my engagement with him. I stated my willingness to be engaged with him and the terms I mentioned were £800 per annum. He said he should not at all object to that but he would prefer to give me £500 certain and to give me an interest in the works by letting me have a percentage on the profits which would probably raise my income to a higher sum than I had mentioned. This I agreed to the principle of, and he promised to let me have a copy of his schedule of prices."*

This seems to have proved satisfactory since in April 1848, in the thick of all the work involved in the contract, Ballard

> *"Made some calculations as to the profits I should derive from my present engagement and it appears that if the contract be finished and the Company pay up I shall get a good fortune that will keep me without further trouble for the remainder of my life."*

In August 1847 he had rented a furnished house at Stilton for £52 a year, including a garden and meadow, but problems with the bog – *"I fear the ground will sink under the weight of the embankment"* – took up his energies. While power pumps removed water, timber rafts were slowly sunk, one on top of the other, weighed down with layers of earth until they reached the bottom of the 22 feet deep bog. On top went the gravel to carry the track.[2] His grandson, Stephen Ballard the Third, noted much later that the task required timber, hurdles and quantities of wheelbarrows.[3]

> *"Stephen Ballard bought up all the coppice wood he could find in the neighbourhood and made it into faggots. These formed the basis of a causeway across the bog."*[4]

On 17th September he seems to have paid his first visit to *"Mr J. Bird of Yaxley"* to whom he made a promise *"to pay all damage we might do in taking materials to the works."* Although no hint of it lies in his journal of 1847, the Bird family was to fill the vacuum in his social life and Mr Bird would eventually become his father-in-law.

Contractors naturally had to be careful that they did not unduly exceed proposed expenditure so routes through difficult terrain constantly presented anxiety. Despite all the problems with the bog, Ballard was able to draw satisfaction from the fact that the section of the route under his superintendence had been achieved economically, thus earning Thomas Brassey's approval and good will. Presumably when he *"had dinner at his house"* in January 1848 it was a very congenial occasion.

In February 1848 he was thrown from his horse and broke his collar-bone, an injury which he did not allow to stop him from paper work in the evening. Within 2 weeks he was able to *"put on*

---

2. Jack Gould *Thomas Brassey,* p.21, Shire Publications, 1975.
3. Stephen Ballard article in 1996 *Newsletter of the Friends of Hereford Record Office.*
4. *Malvern Gazette,* 24th July 1959, Centenary article on the Worcester–Hereford Railway.

my coat for the first time since my accident hurt my shoulder" but his old enemy, depression, took hold once more.

In 1851 Ballard faced the rigours of the Indian climate, having been asked to make the long journey to inspect possible railway routes. This was at the height of the British Raj, only a few years before the Indian Mutiny taught the British to be more sensitive to the religious and social customs of the country they had taken over. Railways, indeed, contributed to the unrest of Indians, who found the consequent mingling of social classes unacceptable to their society, dominated as it was by a rigid caste system. Ballard stayed in India for only a few months before returning to work again with Brassey on a railway between Arnhem and Rotterdam. He spent much of the early 1850s in continental Europe, thus extending his reputation for sound engineering.

Locally, Ballard's chief claim to fame lies in his work as contractor with Brassey and with other engineering staff on the Worcester–Hereford railway line. Boring through the Malvern Hills a tunnel, without which it was impossible to complete the line to Hereford, was a most daunting challenge. One account claims that the Malvern rock was so hard that the best week's work recorded was 2½ yards. This needs some clarification: the total length of the tunnel is 1567 yards and did not take 12 years to complete. The real problem was the central section of solid granite, the stretches of sloping hillside being easier since they involved a mixture of granite and limestone and, on the surfaces, red marl. Even after the tunnel's completion in the summer of 1860 problems remained, with rock falls occurring at air-shafts. By the early 20th century trains sometimes emerged from the tunnel bearing fallen bricks on the roofs of the carriages. Eventually a new tunnel had to be constructed, and the old one served an unusual purpose as an ammunition store during the Second World War. Notwithstanding the difficulties with the tunnel, the railway line transformed the village of Colwall, where Ballard lived: building

Building the first railway tunnel through the Malvern Hills to Ledbury.
Stephen Ballard is believed to be in the dark suit on the right-hand bank.

and property values increased greatly, residents being served by a station which still functions. The official opening of the Colwall tunnel was the occasion for a party of 150 farmers who were carried by train to see the end of the tunnel before sitting down to a typically generous Ballard meal. The more energetic stayed to dance the evening away. The Rev. F Custance, Rector of Colwall, appears not to have dampened enthusiasm too much with his rather solemn exhortation to offer *"thanks to Almighty God for the social and pecuniary benefits of the railway,"* noting that in its

The men responsible for planning and organising the building of the Worcester–Hereford railway line in the 1850s. Left to right: ? Green, ? Whitnall, G. Bird, Robert Ballard, Stephen Ballard, T.W. Baylis, ? Riddler, C. Hall.

construction few accidents had taken place and that *"the short trip they had all so much enjoyed had not been saddened by anything of a melancholy nature."*[5] His comments serve to remind us of both the widespread suspicion with which railways were still regarded and the undoubted dangers encountered by the men who built them. The men themselves, tough and often hard-drinking, were also objects of such suspicion that popular songs urged locals to lock up their daughters when navvies were in the vicinity.

Further down the line the still impressive Ledbury viaduct with its 31 arches was built with 5 million bricks supplied by Ballard's brother, Robert, who had them dug and fired on the

5.   Hereford Record Office: AW86/1

spot.[6] So large a commercial investment in the business of a family member caused – as it did when his brother supplied bricks for the canal – some criticism of Ballard, but the viaduct still stands as tribute to the high standard of work and material.

Ledbury Viaduct (photograph by Bob Embleton © and reproduced with his permission).

There was another very important aspect of Stephen Ballard's contribution to the railway. In the early 1850s he had purchased an estate in Colwall, known as The Winnings. *The Malvern Advertiser,* at the time of his death in 1890, was full of praise for the way in which he promoted the local railway line without himself making a great profit. He had no wish to do as so many landowners had done, when they had demanded huge sums from railway companies wanting to build tracks across their property. Indeed, he is reputed to have told the developers to *"take it at your own price",* an invitation which they must have found quite disarming.

> *"To those who feared that his generosity might be to their pecuniary disadvantage, he declared that so sure was he of the benefit that would ultimately accrue to all by its construction, that he would not hesitate to make a present of his land rather*

6. David E. Bick, *The Hereford and Gloucester Canal and the Gloucester–Ledbury Railway,* p.26, The Pound House, 1979.

    Dictionary of National Biography, Oxford, entry on Stephen Ballard.

than that the project should not be carried out. If the condition of Colwall itself be taken as a criterion, the accuracy of Mr. Ballard's far-sightedness receives striking confirmation – the rateable value of Colwall has more than doubled since the line was opened. … the line is now one of the best paying portions of the vast series of Great Western lines."

During the 1860s Ballard went on to work for the Ashchurch–Evesham, the Evesham–Redditch and the London–Bedford lines. Over the years, all his contractual work gave him responsibility for employing thousands of men,

"not of the highest type viewed from a moral point; but perhaps no employer was regarded with more real respect and affection. The men felt that their master was their friend in whom they could place implicit and unsuspecting trust. Numbers of old employees would from time to time call at The Winnings – some in less prosperous circumstances than aforetime – but many in positions of ease and comfort having worked their way by industry and sobriety. They never called without receiving a hearty greeting followed by thoughtful help when help was needed."

He was known as a thoughtful, generous and kindly employer who earned the respect and affection of his men.

Again, *The Malvern Advertiser* proves a useful source of information, commenting that at the annual Harvest Suppers

"He never omitted the lesson of thrift and prudent saving for times of coming need. As an illustration of his intense desire to benefit the working classes we may point to the Workman's Hall, an institution the like of which, in similar circumstances, is hardly to be met with. … all around, in every direction, are seen striking proofs of his labours of love and disinterested concern for others.

Mr. Ballard was a man of great information and practical knowledge. He made no pretension to the elegancies and polish of a scholar but he had a well informed mind and could take an intelligent part in any conversation, while on subjects that more particularly belonged to his calling he was an authority of a high order. He had also much refinement – he was in fact one of Nature's gentlemen."

Ballard's active work on railways ended in the late 1860s but he continued to work in many spheres for another twenty years, and published a second edition of his pamphlet on *"Cheap Railways"* only a few weeks before his death in November 1890. His own family and estate were naturally particularly close to his heart but he regarded Colwall itself as part of a great extended family, towards which he felt a paternalistic concern consistent with his class and times.

He never forgot his boyhood in Malvern Link and, recognising the special qualities of the Malvern Hills area, he had a passion to conserve the beauty of the countryside surrounding his estate. Although he was described as one of *"Nature's gentlemen"* we should not make the mistake of thinking this rendered him incapable of publicly criticising someone he perceived as the arch enemy of the countryside he loved. She was Malvern's most powerful and respected lady – the Lady of the Manor of Malvern, Lady Emily Foley herself.

V

CONSERVATION

Stephen Ballard played an important role in the establishment of the Malvern Hills Conservators, a body set up in 1884 after much discussion and considerable local acrimony. Given his childhood it was perhaps natural that he should be an enthusiastic supporter of the preservation of the countryside. He knew the history of Malvern's landscape and, having seen it change in the 19th century, feared further irreparable damage.

When in 11th century William the Conqueror established a Royal Forest in this area it is something of a mystery as to why it was known as Malvern Forest, since the seat of administration was 4 miles away in Hanley, then a much more flourishing settlement than Malvern. "Forest" was not merely a description of the landscape but, more importantly, a legal classification of an area subject to special laws designed to protect the hunting rights of the monarch or any favourite to whom he gave rights as "Lord of the Chase."

In the 17th century the financial difficulties of Charles I led him to sell off some of his assets in an attempt to raise money that would enable him to govern without calling parliament. He had Malvern Forest surveyed in 1628, and a disafforestation decree was issued, doing away with forest law. This meant that the king gave up all hunting rights in return for being granted a third of the common land in the old forest area. He wanted money, not land, so it was sold off, and for the first time in five and a half centuries land became legally available for development.

But what is meant by "common land"? Many lawyers have found lucrative pickings, and the hopes of many a poor man have been dashed, in efforts to answer this apparently simple question. To this day there is immense confusion about common land. Clarification lies in understanding the medieval land-holding system. Each parish or manor was controlled by a lord, and was divided in such a way as to enable villagers to cultivate the most fertile land in large communal or common fields, leaving the less fertile land for other purposes. These other purposes included picking nuts and berries, using windfall wood for fuel and house repairs and, probably most important, grazing sheep, cattle and pigs. Often referred to as wasteland, this poorer quality land was for the exclusive use of villagers, who would vigorously defend it against encroachment by inhabitants of neighbouring parishes. Within the area of Malvern Forest, however, inter-commoning was allowed, thus permitting any parish within the forest to enjoy the benefits of the wasteland of all other parishes within the forest boundaries. It was from this wasteland that the king took land which he subsequently sold in order to raise money.

Confusion immediately followed disafforestation and there were riots, eventually quelled by assurances that the remaining two thirds of the wasteland would be left open and free in perpetuity for local inhabitants to use as they always had done. In fact, some encroachment did take place but seems to have been winked at, or even encouraged by local parish authorities. Although the practice was almost certainly illegal, parish authorities were prepared to accept rents for encroachments. Welland, for example, regularly passed resolutions at vestry meetings to sell the crops on any encroachments for which the rent was outstanding. There were also instructions to *"cut up all encroachments that are not paid"* by a specified date. At the same time there was suspicion of the *"pilfering brood"*[1] who set up their hovels on the common.

By the late 18th century, however, anxiety about the future of the wasteland became more acute because rich and powerful landowners sought to enclose great tracts of it by Act of Parliament. The population was increasing, and large property owners were keen to meet the demand for more food by experimenting with new farming methods which were more efficient and offered higher yields. Traditional farming methods were community activities which did not lend themselves to selective breeding or experimentation with new crops. The decision in the late 18th century by two parishes of the former chase – Leigh and Hanley Castle – to enclose their wastes started alarm bells ringing throughout the whole of the chase. For it meant that land over which generations of local inhabitants had exercised common rights was taken into private ownership.

Reduction of the total area of wasteland would obviously have significant repercussions on the common rights of all inhabitants of the former chase. The enclosures, achieved by Acts of Parliament in 1772 and 1795, exacerbated anxiety already aroused by encroachment, an illegal practice easily committed by adjustment of hedgerows by those whose property bordered on the wasteland. The days of turning a blind eye to encroachment were numbered. As long as there was a relatively small population

---

1.   Pamela Hurle, *The Forest and Chase of Malvern,* p.98–9, Phillimore, 2007.

and large tracts of waste, no real problem was perceived, but as the population increased and the waste was whittled away, mutterings became ever louder. Even so, few felt moved to go to the trouble and expense of challenging the culprits in the law courts, probably believing the law would offer little redress. One version of a popular view was clear in its cynicism:

> *"The Law will punish man or woman*
> *Who steals a goose from off the common;*
> *But lets the greater felon loose,*
> *Who steals the common off the goose."*

Anger, resentment and anxiety reached their peak in the Malvern area in the second half of the 19th century, as more parishes sought legal enclosure and encroachment actually seemed to be encouraged by influential landowners. Stephen Ballard was one of the prime campaigners for the preservation of common land, and saw the redoubtable Lady Emily Foley, lady of the manor of Malvern, as a thief stealing the common from the poor. Ballard and Foley were, in fact, remarkably similar – which probably served only to accentuate their loathing of each other.

Lady Emily Graham, daughter of the Duke of Montrose, was born within a few months of Stephen Ballard and married into the Foley family, which lived in Stoke Edith in Herefordshire and had owned the manor of Malvern since 1741. Widowed in 1846, Lady Emily was happy to approve of encroachment – and was perfectly entitled to do so by customs which had been enshrined for centuries in national history. Since medieval times lords of manors had authority over common land and, so long as the needs of local inhabitants were met, any common land surplus to requirements could legally be "approved." This meant that it could be used for any purpose deemed suitable by the lord of the manor. Lady Foley regularly agreed to its use for schools, churches

Lady Emily Foley in her later years.

and working-class housing. Since she approved of the building of Holy Trinity Church and of houses for local workmen in the North Malvern area, her convictions were all too painfully thrust into the consciousness of Stephen Ballard, whose birthplace and boyhood home was just a few yards below these developments. He could not bear to see the erosion of the common, calling it theft from the poor who needed it to graze their animals and enrich their monotonous and frugal diet. This theft also increased the rents collected by the manorial authorities and consolidated their hold over the forelock-tugging workers living in the new cottages in places such as the area called Newtown by late 19th century observers. Ballard wrote in December 1882 to *The Malvern Advertiser:*

"It cannot be doubted that the owner of the manor of Malvern is by far the greatest encroacher – indeed also the only encroacher in what is called the Manor of Malvern. Look at North Malvern ... About 82 valuable houses, with gardens, covering the whole space between the road leading from the Link to Cowleigh. I remember when the whole of this land was open common, free for the use of commoners; now the whole, with the exception, I believe, of two houses, belong to the owner of the Manor. Then there are a number of good houses extending from Newtown to the parsonage of Trinity Church at the top of the Link, all of which stand on land which I remember to be open common land ... The property here and at North Malvern is worth at least £2000 a year. There are many other encroachments now belonging to the same party that I could mention. The manner in which this property has been obtained is very clever; of any other qualities displayed I say nothing but to me the method appears not only unfeeling but cruel. The encroacher, generally a poor man, is allowed without a caution to fence off the common land, to build his hut, and settle himself in his unlawful home; and then he is

frightened into signing an acknowledgement that he occupies land belonging to the owner of the Manor; and further, under the same fear, he agrees to pay a small sum annually in order to live unmolested for a time – that length of time being what the law makes necessary to give a freehold title of his homestead to the owner of the Manor.

Those who are not aware of the great power and influence of the owner of the manor over the inhabitants of Malvern may think it strange that such an extensive pilfering of the common land should have been permitted."

This was strong language but, for her part, Lady Emily could afford to ignore Ballard. She also refused to go through the tunnel which carried the Great Western Railway trains through the Malvern Hills to Herefordshire. It was rumoured that she would have nothing to do with a development so widely perceived as the brainchild of Ballard the engineer. The modern Lady Foley's tea-rooms on Great Malvern Station are so called because they occupy the site of her ladyship's private waiting-room where, having travelled from Stoke Edith by carriage and successfully avoided the smuts and other unpleasant associations of Ballard's tunnel, she awaited the train to carry her eastwards.

Ballard's anger at the erosion of the common, if not his contempt for Lady Foley, was in tune with local feelings and with comments expressed in local newspapers. In September 1858 The Malvern Advertiser carried a letter highlighting the lamentable state of the commons:

"where is the pedestrian in Malvern, who, going up the Worcestershire Beacon has not met with a danger of a special kind.? Who does not know how careful one must be before one indulges in a minute's rest on the soft slopes? There is a large piece of broken plate – there a threatening bit of glass or a bottle."

Twelve years later The Malvern News of 30th April 1870 sought to make the point that the Lady of the Manor of Malvern was ineffectual:

Is there a Manor of Malvern? and if so, who is its lord? Does that lord keep a steward? and where is he to be found? I ask these questions because the commons are in such a wretched condition. Talk about a dung-heap! a mixen! or any place equally filthy and you have an idea of these. Why not keep them in proper order? … Surely these commons might be made places of pleasant resort … Let a committee, self-constituted, set to work to collect subscriptions and expend them in putting in order the commons in this neighbourhood."

During the 19th century Malvern became a fashionable spa for the well-to-do taking the water-cure and, once the railway was built, an attraction for poorer day trippers. This print shows Abbey Road in 1861.

By this time claims of the holders of common rights were being somewhat obscured by other, less justifiable claims. For Malvern had become, from the 1840s, a fashionable spa town whose inhabitants wanted to meet the demands of the affluent middle classes who came for weeks at a time to endure the rigours and the pleasures of hydrotherapy. New boarding-houses and hotels had sprung up, with proprietors eager to preserve the beauties of the landscape for their clientèle to savour. In 1876 the Malvern Hills Preservation Association was set up, and an attempt was made to get through Parliament a bill enabling a group of local representatives to manage the *"hills and commons as an open and free health resort and place of recreation for the public."* Although the Preservation Association declared that it did not want to interfere with any *"vested rights"*, when it drafted a document outlining the main clauses which it thought necessary for inclusion in an Act of Parliament, local tenants, commoners and freeholders were outraged and set about organising a rival camp. The Preservation Association had paid lip-service to *"vested rights"*, but it had failed to grasp their full significance. Those people whose interests had for generations been tied up with the land did not want recreational facilities – their concerns lay in common rights such as grazing, which formed a crucial part of their economic viability. Led by Stephen Ballard and

MALVERN
HILLS & COMMONS
Proposed Act of Parliament.

A MEETING of FREEHOLDERS, TENANTS, and COMMONERS of GREAT MALVERN, COLWALL, and MATHON, will be held at the WORKMAN'S ROOM, COLWALL STONE, on SATURDAY, 11th NOVEMBER, at 3 o'clock, for the purpose of discussing the advantages or disadvantages of the BILL which is proposed (vesting the Hills and Commons in a body of Malvern Conservators), when the attendance of PERSONS interested in the subject is invited.

**STEPHEN BALLARD,
JOHN CHEESE,
HENRY LAKIN,
R. W. RAPER.**

Dated November 4th, 1882.

Poster advertising the meeting that led to the first Malvern Hills Act of 1884.

a neighbouring academic called Robert Raper, together with John Cheese and Henry Lakin, a surveyor who had in 1881 challenged an encroachment at Barnard's Green, they called a public meeting on 11th November 1882 to discuss the bill proposed by the Preservation Association. The eventual outcome of this was the drafting of an entirely new bill which was to become the First Malvern Hills Act of 1884, setting up the Malvern Hills Conservators. Remarkably generous and innovative, this Act encompassed not only the preservation of ancient common rights but also insisted on giving public access to the hills and commons for recreational purposes. The Conservators were given a very difficult task in reconciling the needs of farmers and pleasure seekers but the two groups shared one basic priority – the preservation of common land and constant vigilance against enclosure and encroachment.

Two important points need to be made here. The first is to make absolutely clear that the old myth that the Conservators were founded to prevent quarrying on the hills is just that – a myth. The problems of quarrying belong to a later chapter of the history of the Conservators who were founded to stop the erosion of the common land. This was a constant theme in the thinking of Stephen Ballard, whose role as a respected elder statesman was vital in formulating the opposition to any act which failed adequately to address that problem. The historic 11th November meeting took place in the very hall which he had built for the people of Colwall.

The second point is that the *vested rights* were not solely those of the commoners. There were also lords of manors who had vested rights and were keen to make sure that they kept them. They – the likes of Lady Foley and the Hornyold family – had to be satisfied that the new body would not infringe their traditional rights. Herein lay more opportunity for Stephen Ballard and Lady Foley to cross swords.

From this point Stephen Ballard, now an old man, was a less significant player than Robert Raper and his lawyer associates. Nevertheless, Ballard can take much of the credit for the 1884 Malvern Hills Act which set up the Malvern Hills Conservators who were given the task of keeping open the hills and commons around Malvern for the benefit not only of the holders of traditional common rights, but also to provide opportunities for the general public to have access to the land. Allowing such access to the general public was a pioneering policy in the last quarter of the 19th century and led to some conflict of interest, which was soon to be shown when in the late 1880s Queen Victoria's Golden Jubilee was marked by the construction of a carriageway from British Camp to the Wyche Cutting.

This construction of Jubilee Drive was the last of Stephen Ballard's remarkable achievements, officially opened in October 1889. The work was supervised by the Conservators' ranger, Alexander King, but Ballard contributed some of his land as well as his engineering expertise in order to realise his 30 year old dream of such a road. It was, however, seen by his opponents as a betrayal of commoners, since it cut through valuable common land, depriving farmers of about 10 acres of useful grazing and causing inconvenience by cutting through particularly good ground. Perceived by them as pandering to pleasure seekers, the road illustrates how delicate is the balance which the Conservators have always striven to achieve between the interests of those exercising common rights and the interests of those seeking relaxation. It is now so difficult to imagine the hills without Jubilee Drive that the ill-feeling it generated at the time of its being built comes as something of a shock.

Timber going through the Wyche Cutting – a late 19th century picture.

Jubilee Drive at the end of the 19th century.

VI

MARRIAGE AND
LIFE AT THE WINNINGS

In 1854 Stephen Ballard married, at the age of 50, Maria Bird who was exactly half his age. This considerable difference in their ages was the focus of some discussion before the marriage, but at least one of her family friends had nothing but praise for an older husband. Her own was 17 years older than she and she recommended *"the older one every time."* Maria and Stephen's marriage lasted for over 36 years, until his death in 1890 and, surviving him by nearly 25 years, she never remarried. In 1947 their daughter Ada, then aged 85, recalled

> *"I had a goodly heritage in that both of my parents were to me ideal examples of parenthood. … It was a perfect match, father always young for his years, and mother rather sedate and solemn, made them a balanced couple. Father loved a joke; mother had no sense of humour. I have seen his eyes twinkle when some joke or funny tale was repeated by him, and mother's face remained immovable."*

Ballard met his wife when he was working with Brassey on the Great Northern railway. Two years before the marriage he had thought long and hard about a business contract which would have taken him abroad, but turned it down for fear of losing the chance to marry. Maria's father, John Bird, was a prominent farmer in the village of Yaxley, near Peterborough. He was convinced of the importance of proper drainage and, like Stephen Ballard, he showed great commitment to the community, working to ensure that Yaxley had its own village school, as well as chairing a number of local enterprises. Maria was a very dutiful and serious minded daughter who, two days after her quiet Yaxley wedding to Ballard in April 1854,[1] wrote to her parents a most intriguing letter, which dispels any notion of the marriage being an impulsive or light-hearted undertaking by a young and carefree girl:

"An uncertain future is of course before me but I sincerely trust although trials may await me I shall bear them as cheerfully as I can, and I feel assured I shall have the sympathy of the one I've chosen. I have no doubt of his kindness and affection, still I'm well aware that many think us unsuited to each other. I cannot comment but know prayer will do much.

Maria Ballard

---

1. Stephen Ballard's wedding outfit, in Malvern Museum, shows that he was quite a short man.

In the last few months it has been a struggle to think of leaving you all, and at one time I thought it amounted to ingratitude to think of forsaking those who have done so much for me.

I heartily trust I may never repent my choice. I only hope I may have the inexpressible pleasure of seeing you at my new home, and I don't despair of seeing some of your kind faces in Holland.

Ever believe me the same fond affectionate and grateful child Maria."

They went almost immediately to Holland because he had just accepted a Dutch contract for the Arnheim–Rotterdam railway. Like her letter, Maria's diary shows a maturity and perception which was probably one of her attractions to her middle-aged bridegroom. She found French politeness only skin-deep, was impressed by 350 men working on Cologne Cathedral and recorded the extraordinary value of the shrine of the Three Kings – six million francs. On 3rd June they viewed their future home facing the canal around Utrecht, moving into it on the 6th. Within a few days they were off to Amsterdam, Rotterdam, Gouda and The Hague. For nearly two years they travelled around Holland: from the top of the King's Palace in Amsterdam Maria could see 1600 windmills and was *"much struck by the beauty of the country and the gardens and tidy cottages."* Perhaps it was such experiences which encouraged her husband to pay careful attention to the building of cottage homes on his Colwall estate some years later. A wife much younger than her husband probably found it easy to adopt the 19th century formality with which husbands and wives referred to each other: Maria noted that *"Mr Ballard"* had work to do. Clearly, however, he had more time to relax than he ever seemed to have had before.

Maria was not especially impressed by the Palace in the Wood at The Hague, dismissing it as *"not very royal, full of Japanese and Chinese furnishings and paintings."* In January 1855 she went to a concert with friends and noted that *"Madame Schumann, the celebrated pianist performed beautifully".* Ten days later she went to a concert in Utrecht where she *"heard Jenny Goldschmidt."* This is of special interest since Madame Goldschmidt was better known as Jenny Lind, the "Swedish Nightingale", who actually spent her final years at Wind's Point, a mile away from the Ballard home in Colwall.

The line from Utrecht to Gouda was opened on 21st May. On 29th May Maria went with a group to Haarlem and, without use of full-stops, wrote of the journey *"to look at a proposed canal across the sand hills to save the distance ships have to travel in order to reach Amsterdam ... I was left as a landmark, upon a hill that they might know which way to turn back, in such a wild country one might easily be lost, it was a strange sight to see such an immense tract of country uninhabited, composed of nothing but sand hills, blown up by the wind."* Although she found Antwerp Cathedral spire *"the most beautiful in Europe"* she did not approve of the Virgin Mary being carried in procession through the town. Maria was, after all, the woman who was later to join the non-conformist Countess of Huntingdon's Connexion after she settled down with her husband in Colwall.

Two weeks in England in the summer of 1855 included a visit to see at Sydenham the Crystal Palace in which the Great Exhibition had been held four years previously. On 30th September the Ballards went back to Holland for a further three months, then *"very cheerfully bid adieu to its shores"* and took up residence in Colwall, on the extensive farm estate which Stephen had bought. He designed a large new, comfortable, centrally heated home – The Winnings. With their customary thought for the unfortunate it had a large back porch with seats for the poor who came to ask for a bowl of soup. From this house Stephen Ballard was to work on the Worcester–Hereford railway line and, on the surrounding estate, put to good effect the horticultural and building skills learned in his youth.

Maria bore Stephen four sons and four daughters. Ada Ballard remembered the

Outside The Winnings, a trap drawn by a donkey.

A more up-market form of transport – a horse-drawn carriage as used by Maria Ballard until she purchased one of the early motor-cars.

"lovely winter evenings in the old home. … Father would have my four brothers in the library, and talk to them on subjects which were going to help them … farming, building, nature and drainage. … And what of we four girls? We sat with my mother in another room, each with her work-box or basket, making garments under her instruction for the poor of the parish, and they were poor in those days. While we sewed mother read to us – lovely books – she was a beautiful reader. I remember her reading 'Jane Eyre' and being reproved by one of her friends who thought it not quite a suitable book to read to young people.

My father used to offer sixpence every year to the one who first heard the cuckoo. We were always disappointed in winning the prize by his saying at the breakfast table 'I heard the cuckoo this morning.' He was an early riser and until the last year of his life was always out in the garden before breakfast. How fond he was of nature; as soon as I could hold

Two old views of Colwall.

a spade I was given a little patch of ground to cultivate. How well I remember my first bed of carrots – and my little flower garden with a tiny rockery of ferns at the end. I can hear his voice now as he came round the garden and saw me at work, then with a pat on my shoulder he would say, 'Well done, little gardener.' Always ready to praise and encourage. ... I never remember my father raising his voice, I never saw him angry – so calm, so gentle and yet so strong. I can't ever remember wanting to disobey him."

The children did not disobey their mother either but

"Mother seldom, if ever, commended us. She had a difficult team to drive in we eight children, but how skilfully she did it. We hardly realised we were being controlled, and yet she let us each develop our own special characteristics."

In addition to the domestic duties which a large family laid upon her, Maria worked to support her husband when, after retiring from his engineering work, he concentrated on developing the Colwall estate based on The Winnings and including the nearby Grovesend and The Court. Vast quantities of produce were preserved in the summer and autumn: their daughter, Fanny Ballard, in her diaries mentioned 176 pounds of summer fruit being preserved in 1879, to be followed by quantities of plums and apples in the autumn of that year. Ballard employees were well paid and cared for in a more generous way than was the norm. A special occasion each year was the Harvest Supper.

"What an event was the Harvest Home Supper every Autumn, held in the granaries of the Winnings Farm at 6 o'clock. The guests, some 300, arrived and sat down to a real English dinner of roast and boiled beef and mutton, plum pudding, apple pies and rice pudding. Then came the toasts to Queen Victoria, and the British Workman, followed by a talk by father generally on 'thrift'. At 9 o'clock the tables were removed and dancing began. The first was a country dance called 'The Triumph' led off by father and Mrs. Bright – and Timbrell, the bricklayer and his wife. … Only one year did we exceed the time of closing (12 o'clock) because my father's watch had stopped."

Ballard was a good and considerate employer. His grandson cited the words of the woodman, James Ecock, speaking at a harvest supper:

*Stephen and Maria Ballard with their four sons and four daughters in the 1880s.
Back row from the left: Gertrude, Stephen junior, Mary, George;
middle row Fred, Maria, Stephen, Fanny; front row Ernest, Ada.*

*Stephen Ballard's tree transplanter. It is probably Ballard himself
standing in the doorway of one of the houses on his Colwall estate.*

The scene set for one of the popular Harvest suppers given by the Ballard family.

"A man like Mr Ballard will not see a labourer fall down and leave him, he will reach out his hand to help him. There would not be any need for trades unions if only people would follow Mr Ballard's example."[2]

Some local farmers did not approve of Ballard's attitude to farming and to his employees – his grandson claimed that they burnt an effigy of him on Colwall Green – but he was determined to run his estate using innovative and humane methods. He preferred square fields of about 12 acres for arable farming, using stationary engines and cables rather than horses for ploughing, in order to avoid compacting the soil. The granaries at The Winnings, where harvest suppers were held, were part of his ambitious plans. Two galleries, 150 feet long, ran each side of

---

2. Stephen Ballard, *Colwall Collection*, p.45, 1999.

a central bay over cow and horse stalls.[3] Another of his ideas concerned silage making on which, in December 1884 *The Malvern Advertiser* wrote at length, since it was seen as a means of helping farmers with animal feeding costs at a time when farming was in depression. Ballard and his sons had built at The Winnings a silo designed to hold 70 tons of clover and maize and at his Grovesend property one to hold 30 tons. The feed could be produced at a cost of 9d (less than 4p) a ton.

He built 17 houses in Colwall,[4] his use of concrete being innovative and attracting wide interest. Malvern spring water used for domestic supplies laid the foundation for the Schweppes bottling industry in the village. He also laid out some 3 miles of roads, his most noteworthy being Jubilee Drive which, as already indicated, to some locals seemed contrary to what he had sought to do in the establishment of the Malvern Hills Conservators.

In the early 1880s Stephen Ballard built the Workman's Hall so that working men would have an alcohol-free meeting place. It was at the Workman's Hall in November 1882 that the historic – some say riotous – meeting was held that led to the foundation of the Malvern Hills Conservators. Ballard also built the Colwall Temperance Hotel to please his wife and daughters who were stalwart supporters of the Temperance Movement and its belief in the slogan "Water is best". In their campaigns based on the Band of Hope which flourished in Colwall under their guidance, they sought to remove the great temptation of alcohol, which was undoubtedly responsible for much poverty and unhappiness, particularly in working-class families. Memories of his own childhood probably encouraged Stephen Ballard's support of his wife and daughters. (With the help of her sons Stephen and Ernest, Maria and her daughters Ada and Mary later built two

---

3.   Ibid, p.44
4.   Notes by his grandson, Stephen Ballard.

evangelical chapels in Colwall, one in the village and the other, known as the Wyche Free Church, higher up the hill at the Wyche end of Jubilee Drive.)[5]

Ballard sought to provide for his large family in ways that brought employment to the village. Another of his schemes was the Vinegar Works, successor to the Ledbury one at which his son Stephen had worked. It produced high quality vinegar for some 30 years until bought out in 1914 by Fardons of Birmingham, who ceased production at the site in Stone Drive.[6]

Like her husband, who was a compassionate Overseer of the poor for many years, Maria was much concerned with those less fortunate than herself. Her good works included provision of

Wyche Mission Chapel

5. Stephen Ballard, *Colwall Collection*, p.52, 1999.

6. Ibid, p.20–3

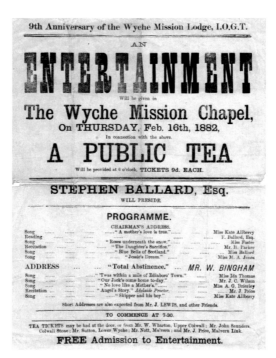

Programme for tea and entertainment at the Wyche Chapel.

The Upper Wyche in the early 20th century.

herbal remedies for a wide range of infirmities. One request for help came from the wife of one of the Winnings estate workers:

> *"Please could Mrs Ballard send iei loishon for iei have a very bad iei. It is red has fire and very paneful. iei have been bathing it with milk and water but it duse no good."*

Ada recorded

> *"Mother was very clever with medicines. Our doctor lived five miles away at Ledbury. There was no railway until 1862, no nurse or chemist, so Mother furnished a cupboard with more than 50 medicines, together with bandages, etc. and the village people came to her for advice. I remember seeing her sew up a bad gash in a workman's hand. She was also a great caterer and her skill in this direction was often required for the many public functions in which my father was interested."*

Sometimes Maria's efforts to raise money fell upon deaf ears, but it must have come as a particularly unpleasant surprise to receive from her banker neighbour, James Martin of Old Colwall, the following reply to a request for help in June 1867:

> *"Dear Mrs Ballard,*
> *Thank you for your note of yesterday's date and for your opinion of my disposition to be kind to my fellow creatures, however unfounded it may be.*
> *I think the people in London are quite rich enough to take care of their own poor and if they won't I won't help them whatever you may do. I think we had better look at home where we can find out if it is really wanted and deserved. Indiscriminate liberality encourages much imposition, and does much mischief.*
> *If you, however, like many others only give away your money to save your souls and that your name may appear in*

the subscription before God and Man the object is answered
no matter where the money goes. I don't believe this of you but
want you not to allow yourself to be imposed on by this wicked
world or let them pick your pockets while they are melting your
timorous heart.

With my best regards to Mr Ballard when you see him,
which I believe you never do.

Believe me yours sincerely,
James Martin."

This reference to Ballard's absence presumably relates to the need for him to be away on railway work. The letter also indicates that, despite – or perhaps because of – all that Ballard did for Colwall and his workers, he and his family were not entirely popular with other middle class families in the village. The family's relationship with the parish church seems also to have been somewhat strained. Maria and her daughters worshipped with the Countess of Huntingdon's Connexion, while the sons walked to the parish churches of Little Malvern, Coddington and Mathon. It all bears comparison with the experiences of Lady Henry Somerset in nearby Eastnor: she was criticised by clergy and laity when she tried to help the poor, being described as a traitor to her class. She, like Maria Ballard, was also deeply concerned about the effects of drunkenness on individuals and their families, and passionately supported the temperance movements which developed in the 19th century.

Ballard's concern for the poor was shown in his letter to The Daily News in February 1886 – one of the coldest months of the year – advocating the provision of a cheap and nourishing soup:

"I was glad to see in The Daily News today that attention
is directed to the waste of broken food in the houses of the rich
and well to do.

Stephen Ballard in 1888.

Maria Ballard in old age.

I have for many years saved such foods as is generally thrown into the hogs' tub for the pigs and my experience may be of use to those who desire to help the poor.

My residence is by the high-road used by workmen travelling between Wales and the mining and manufacturing district of Staffordshire, and a great many men, women and children travel on this road.

Over 5800 basins of soup a year are given to the hungry poor at my back door. The plan adopted is this: a large stock pot is constantly in use on the kitchen fire range. Into this pot scraps of meat, bones, gravies and other edible scraps of provisions are put and then thoroughly stewed; thickening of rice, split peas with salt and pepper are added and the result is a savoury and nutritious soup.

All scraps and crusts of bread are saved. They are generally not sufficient for the soup and some bread which might be used otherwise is required but now the cost of bread is little.

A very considerable amount of extra work is entailed on the cook, not only in making the soup but mainly in giving it away to the hungry applicants. This extra labour the cook cheerfully submits to, working people generally have a kind and charitable feeling for those who are in want.

Some objections are made to this method of helping the starving poor on account of the danger of encouraging regular tramps that never will work. Occasionally such idle impostors may be supplied but only a small proportion of the whole. Most of those supplied are working men, out of work and are worthy objects of charity. The fear of erring by encouraging an occasional idle tramp I think should not prevent the practice of saving food from waste now the very great proportion travelling are without doubt working men.

If the head of any establishment would examine the tub in which the pigs' food is put he would find that much good food is wasted. Then let him consider whether he is justified in permitting undue waste while so many are suffering from the want of food and when at a trifling cost he might supply a large quantity of food to the poor in need."

In October 1887 when Ballard was 83, he must have been deeply shocked by the murder of his older brother, Philip, who was an artist. His own daughter, Ada, was staying with her uncle when burglars entered his house in Tupsley and murdered the well-respected old man. Two men were hanged for the murder.

When Stephen Ballard died in November 1890 he left his estate of £130,000 to Maria on trust, the administrators being their two sons, Fred and Stephen the Second. He was buried in a secluded spot on his Colwall estate, close to the ventilation shaft of the railway tunnel he had built.

Four hundred mourners attended his funeral – another indication of how highly he was regarded. When The Malvern Advertiser described him as one of *"Nature's gentlemen"*, it also printed Coleridge's surprisingly modern sounding comment that *"the greatest men are those in whom something of the beauty of the feminine nature is conjoined with the sterner qualities of the masculine nature"*. In Stephen Ballard, added the newspaper, *"the two were happily blended."*

One mourner wrote to *The Malvern Advertiser* that, although he was

"not of loud religious profession, nor busy in his dance upon services and sacraments, his life was a tuneful poem, unerring in its integrity."

He never flinched from

"the path of exact rectitude. … A sagacious, prudent, wise and successful man … he remained to the last simple, unostentatious and lowly."

Stephen Ballard was clearly an exceptional man.

The burial place of Stephen and Maria Ballard. On private land close to the tunnel ventilation shaft, it is also the final resting place of several of their relations.

BIBLIOGRAPHY

Ballard Collection in Hereford Record Office.

Ballard records in private ownership.

Stephen Ballard, Article in 1996 *Newsletter of Friends of Hereford Record Office.*

Stephen Ballard, *Colwall Collection,* Weaver, 1999.

David E. Bick, *The Hereford and Gloucester Canal and the Gloucester–Ledbury Railway,* The Pound House, 1979.

Jack Gould, *Thomas Brassey,* Shire Publications, 1975.

Pamela Hurle, *Beneath the Malvern Hills,* 1973.

Pamela Hurle, *The Forest and Chase of Malvern,* Phillimore, 2007.

Institution of Civil Engineers, Obituary of Stephen Ballard.

The *Malvern Advertiser,* Various editions, but especially 22nd November 1890.

The *Malvern Gazette,* 24th July 1959.

The *Malvern News,* 30th April 1870.

Turberville, T.C., *Worcestershire in the 19th century,* Longman, Brown, Green and Longmans, 1852.

G.C. Warren, *From an Engineer's Diary 1845–1848.* Article written for *Huntingdon Local History Association.*

Philip Weaver, *Ballard, Stephen (1804–1890), Dictionary of National Biography,* O.U.P., 2008.